T0387502

The Solar System

LEVEL 11

DECODABLES BY jump!

Teaching Tips

Lime Level 11
This book focuses on developing reading independence, fluency, and comprehension.

Before Reading
- Ask readers what they think the book will be about based on the title. Have them support their answer.

Read the Book
- Encourage readers to read silently on their own.
- As readers encounter unfamiliar words, ask them to look for context clues to see if they can figure out what the words mean. Encourage them to locate boldfaced words in the glossary and ask questions to clarify the meaning of new vocabulary.
- Allow readers time to absorb the text and think about each chapter.
- Ask readers to write down any questions they have about the book's content.

After Reading
- Ask readers to summarize the book.
- Encourage them to point out anything they did not understand and ask questions.
- Ask readers to review the questions on page 23. Have them go back through the book to find answers. Have them write their answers on a separate sheet of paper.

North American adaptations © 2024 Jump!
5357 Penn Avenue South
Minneapolis, MN 55419
www.jumplibrary.com

Library of Congress Cataloging-in-Publication Data is available at www.loc.gov or upon request from the publisher.

ISBN: 979-8-88996-957-0 (hardcover)
ISBN: 979-8-88996-958-7 (paperback)
ISBN: 979-8-88996-959-4 (ebook)

Photo Credits

Images are courtesy of Shutterstock.com. With thanks to Getty Images, Thinkstock Photo and iStockphoto. Cover – robert_s, Pike-28, Photoongraphy. 4–5 – cigdem, markeusz. 6–7 – NDanko Arthur Balitskii. 8–9 – Triff, Vadim Sadovski. 10–11 – Castleski. 12–13 – John T Takai, Christos Georghiou. 14–15 – John T Takai, Christos Georghiou. 16–17 – Tom Whitfield, Wirestock Creators. 18–19 – Johan Swanepoel, vchal. 20–21 – critterbiz, Anatolii Vasilev.

Table of Contents

The Solar System

The solar system is the Sun and all the objects that move around it. The way these objects move around the Sun is called an **orbit**. Eight planets orbit the Sun, including Earth. There are also many moons, dwarf planets, and asteroids in our solar system.

Sun

In the past, people thought everything orbited planet Earth. They believed Earth was the center of the universe. We now know this is not true. Everything in our solar system orbits the Sun. The solar system is even named after the Sun! "Solar" means to do with the Sun.

Copernicus figured out that the planets actually orbit the Sun.

Gravity

Every object that orbits the Sun is held there by gravity. Gravity is all around us, but we cannot see it. Gravity means that all objects pull on each other, and this is how they stay in place.

Earth's gravity pulls objects toward it.

Earth has gravity. Earth's gravity pulls objects toward the center of Earth. This makes sure that objects stay on Earth and do not float into outer space. If you drop something, it will always fall to the ground. This is because gravity pulls the object down toward Earth's center.

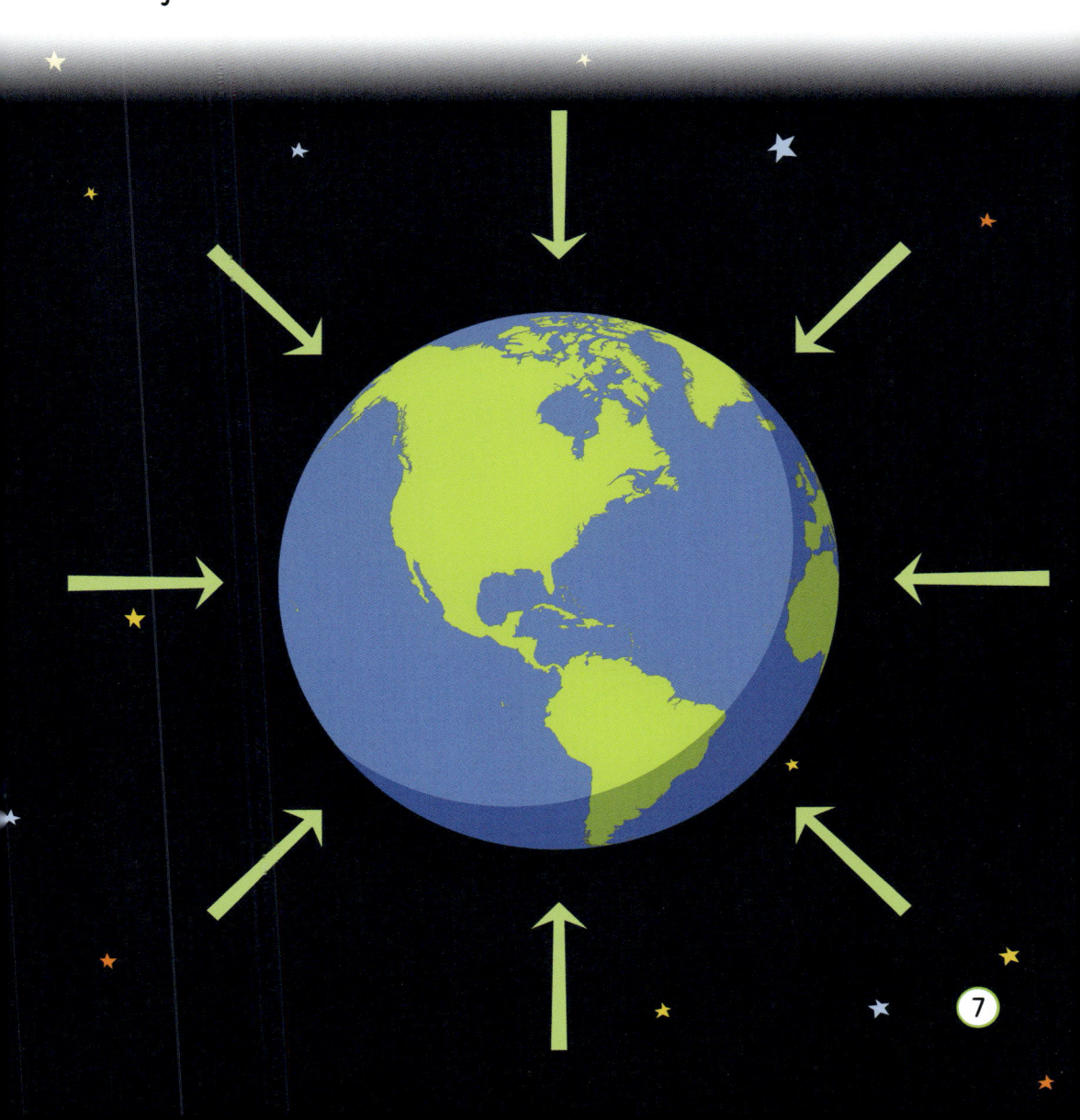

The Sun

The Sun is a star. Stars are giant balls of flaming gas. They are very hot and bright. The Sun is very large, but there are many other stars in other solar systems that are much larger. To us, the Sun appears to be the biggest star, but this is only because it is the closest star to our planet.

The Sun heats and lights all the planets in our solar system. The Sun is very hot, but only a tiny amount of the Sun's heat reaches Earth. The light that comes from the Sun takes around eight minutes to reach Earth. We need the Sun to live. It keeps the planet warm and helps plants grow.

The Moon

The Moon is a large ball of rock that orbits Earth. The Moon is spherical, which means it is round like a ball. From Earth, it looks like the Moon changes shape at different times of the month. This is because the Moon does not make any light, so we can only see the bits of the Moon that are lit by the Sun.

The phases of the Moon

Apart from Earth, scientists know more about the Moon than any other object in our solar system. Because the Moon is quite close to Earth, it is easier to learn about than planets. **Astronauts** have even landed and walked on the Moon! There are footprints left on the Moon by astronauts.

Footprints

The Planets

The planets are the largest objects that orbit the Sun. Planets are made of rock or gas. Each planet is **unique** and has a different path around the Sun. This way, the planets never bump into each other. These paths are called orbital paths.

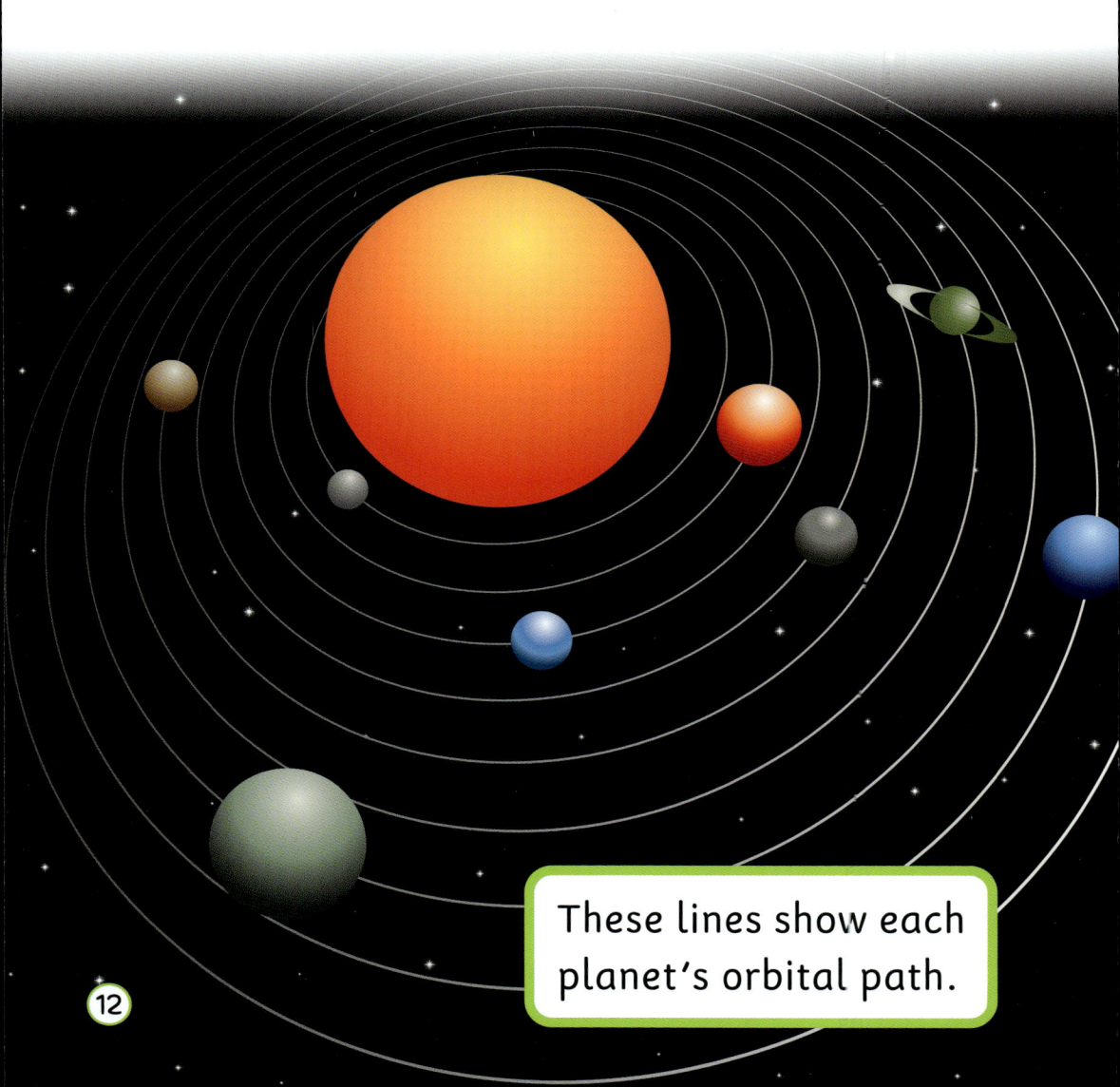

These lines show each planet's orbital path.

The planets in our solar system are Mercury, Venus, Earth, Mars, Jupiter, Saturn, Uranus, and Neptune. Scientists used to call Pluto the ninth planet. However, in 2006 they realized Pluto is actually a dwarf planet. Dwarf planets are similar to planets but are much smaller.

Earth

Pluto

Earth

Earth is the planet we live on. It is about 93 million miles away from the Sun. Earth is made mostly of rock. It is the largest rocky planet in the solar system.

Earth is the only planet known to have life on it. It has water on its surface, which is needed to support life. Earth is also the right distance away from the Sun. This means it has the right temperature for plants and animals to survive. The parts of Earth's surface that are not covered by water have mountains, flat land, deserts, and **canyons**.

The Stars

The Sun is the only star in our solar system. From Earth, we can see many stars beyond our solar system. The solar system is inside the universe. There are millions of stars and many other solar systems in the universe. However, they are very far away, so we do not know as much about them.

A group of stars is called a galaxy. Galaxies are very large and have billions of stars. There are lots of galaxies in space. Our solar system is part of a galaxy called the Milky Way. The closest galaxy to the Milky Way is the Andromeda Galaxy.

Milky Way

What Else Is Out There?

Outer space is very large, so much of it has not been **explored**. Even though there is a lot left to explore, scientists have found lots of interesting things in space. Asteroids are pieces of rock that orbit the Sun. Some asteroids orbit the Sun together in an asteroid belt.

Asteroids

Have you ever heard of a shooting star? Shooting stars are actually meteorites. Meteorites are smaller objects that start in space and make it through a planet's **atmosphere** to the surface. The light we see when a meteorite falls to Earth is caused by heat around the meteorite.

Some stars form patterns. These patterns are called constellations.

Alien Life

People have often wondered whether Earth is the only planet that has life. For life to exist, it needs water and the right amount of heat. When scientists explore new planets and moons, they look for water. They have not yet found any other planets that are like Earth.

There are countless planets outside our solar system. Could there be one that is just the right distance from a star to support life like Earth is? Scientists have discovered more than 3,200 stars that have orbiting planets. Do you think there could be life on another planet?

Index

asteroids 4, 18

astronauts 11

constellations 19

Copernicus 5

dwarf planets 4, 13

meteorites 19

Milky Way 17

orbit 4–6, 10, 12, 18, 21

universe 5, 16

water 15, 20

How to Use an Index

An index helps us find information in a book. Each word has a set of page numbers. These page numbers are where you can find information about that word.

Page numbers

Example: balloons 5, 8–10, 19

Important word

This means page 8, page 10, and all the pages in between. Here, it means pages 8, 9, and 10.

Questions

1. How many minutes does it take for light from the Sun to reach Earth?

2. Why does it look like the Moon changes shape throughout the month?

3. Shooting stars are not really stars. What are they?

4. Using the Table of Contents, can you find what page you can read about gravity?

5. Using the Index, can you find a page in the book about the Milky Way?

6. Using the Glossary, can you define who astronauts are?

Glossary

astronauts:
People who travel to space.

atmosphere:
The mass of gases that surrounds a planet.

canyons:
Narrow, deep valleys that have steep sides.

explored:
To have traveled and discovered things.

orbit:
One object's path around another.

unique:
One of a kind.